THE LITTLE BOOK OF

UNITED STATES PRESIDENTS

Published by Orange Hippo!
20 Mortimer Street
London W1T 3JW

Text © 2020 Orange Hippo!
Design © 2020 Orange Hippo!

Disclaimer:
All trademarks, quotations, company names, registered names,
products, characters, logos and catchphrases used or cited in
this book are the property of their respective owners. This book
is a publication of *OH! An imprint of Welbeck Publishing Group
Limited* and has not been licensed, approved, sponsored, or
endorsed by any person or entity.

All rights reserved. No part of this publication may be reproduced,
stored in a retrieval system, or transmitted in any form or by any
means (including electronic, mechanical, photocopying, recording,
or otherwise) without prior written permission from the publisher.

ISBN 978-1-91161-051-9

Editorial: Jenn Arnott, Victoria Godden
Project manager: Russell Porter
Design: Darren Jordan
Production: Rachel Burgess

A CIP catalogue for this book is available from the British Library

Printed in Dubai

10 9 8 7 6 5 4 3 2 1

Cover photograph: Moe Sasi/Shutterstock

THE LITTLE BOOK OF

UNITED STATES PRESIDENTS

IN THEIR OWN WORDS

CONTENTS

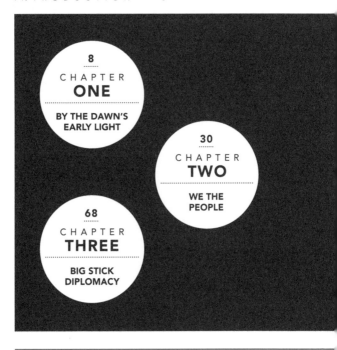

INTRODUCTION

The office of President was created out of the needs of an unstable union, trying in earnest to pull together and create a government for thirteen sovereign states; a light freed from the shadow of colonialism.

Upon the ratification of the Constitution, the role was set – the President would be the head of the Executive branch, leading with the promise to "take care the laws be faithfully executed." Most importantly the President was elected, not forced on the people by birthright.

The rules are simple – to be considered for the office the candidate must be a natural-born citizen of the United States, over the age of 35 and a resident in the country for more than 14 years.

From George Washington to the 45th President, Donald Trump, the nation's leaders have come from all walks of life. A number of military figures and career civil servants have held the post. Some seem born to the position, while others have had it thrust upon them by unfortunate circumstance. The White House has been home to adventurers, teachers and actors alike.

Whatever their background, each President inherits a responsibility to the people of the United States – and in more recent times, the world – to lead in the face of crisis, fight back in the face of evil, and inspire in times of struggle.

As George Washington put it, "There is scarcely any action, whose motives may not be subject to a double interpretation. There is scarcely any part of my conduct which may not hereafter be drawn into precedent."

When the President speaks the world is listening and taking note. This collection of over 170 inspiring and thought-provoking quotations spans the tenure of each President, and the messages can be taken to heart by anyone who has ever truly loved their nation and their people.

CHAPTER
ONE

Rather than be ruled by a monarch and government an ocean away, the Founding Fathers declared independence and set out to create the framework for a new government and nation led by the people and for the people.

BY THE DAWN'S EARLY LIGHT

It is by a thorough knowledge of the whole subject that our fellow-citizens are enabled to judge correctly of the past and to give a proper direction to the future.

JAMES MONROE (5TH)
Democratic-Republican, March 4, 1817 – March 4, 1825

Second Inaugural Address, March 5, 1821

I am moved by no other impulse than a most earnest desire for the perpetuation of that Union which has made us what we are, showering upon us blessings and conferring a power and influence which our fathers could hardly have anticipated, even with their most sanguine hopes directed to a far-off future.

FRANKLIN PIERCE (14TH)
Democratic, March 4, 1853 – March 4, 1857

Inaugural Address, March 4, 1853

The true strength of our nation comes not from the might of our arms or the scale of our wealth, but from the enduring power of our ideals: democracy, liberty, opportunity, and unyielding hope.

BARACK OBAMA (44TH)
Democratic, January 20, 2009 – January 20, 2017

Election victory speech, Chicago, Illinois, November 4, 2008

If there is anything which is dear to Americans, which they are bound to preserve at all hazards, it is their independence.

CALVIN COOLIDGE (30TH)
Republican, August 2, 1923 – March 4, 1929

Dedicating a monument to the First Division, American Expeditionary Forces, Washington DC, October 4, 1924

The hope of freedom itself depends, in real measure, upon our strength, our heart, and our wisdom.

DWIGHT D. EISENHOWER (34TH)
Republican, January 20, 1953 – January 20, 1961

1953 State of the Union Address

When legislature is corrupted,
the people are undone.

JOHN ADAMS (2ND)
Federalist, March 4, 1797 – March 4, 1801

America, with the same voice which spoke herself into existence as a nation, proclaimed to mankind the inextinguishable rights of human nature, and the only lawful foundations of government.

JOHN QUINCY ADAMS (6TH)
Democratic-Republican, March 4, 1825 – March 4, 1829

Speech to the US House of Representatives on foreign policy, July 4, 1821

"

Amid all the clash of conflicting interests, amid all the welter of partisan politics, every American can turn for solace and consolation to the Declaration of Independence and the Constitution of the United States with the assurance and confidence that those two great charters of freedom and justice remain firm and unshaken.

"

CALVIN COOLIDGE (30TH)
Republican, August 2, 1923 – March 4, 1929

**"The Inspiration of the Declaration" speech,
July 5, 1926**

All too will bear in mind this sacred principle, that though the will of the majority is in all cases to prevail, that will, to be rightful, must be reasonable; that the minority possess their equal rights, which equal laws must protect, and to violate would be oppression.

THOMAS JEFFERSON (3RD)
Democratic-Republican, March 4, 1801 – March 4, 1809

First Inaugural Address, March 4, 1801

In imitating their example I tread in the footsteps of illustrious men, whose superiors it is our happiness to believe are not found on the executive calendar of any country.

MARTIN VAN BUREN (8TH)
Democratic, March 4, 1837 – March 4, 1841

Inaugural Address, March 4, 1837

…the whole action of the Government instituted by it should be invariably and sacredly devoted – to form a more perfect union, establish justice, insure domestic tranquillity, provide for the common defense, promote the general welfare, and secure the blessings of liberty to the people of this Union in their successive generations.

JOHN QUINCY ADAMS (6TH)
Democratic-Republican, March 4, 1825 – March 4, 1829

Inaugural Address, March 4, 1825

Liberty, once lost, is lost forever.

JOHN ADAMS (2ND)

Federalist, March 4, 1797 – March 4, 1801

Letter to Abigail Adams, July 17, 1775

But be this as it may, it is the imperative and indispensable duty of the Government of the United States to secure to every resident inhabitant the free and independent expression of his opinion by his vote. This sacred right of each individual must be preserved.

JAMES BUCHANAN (15TH)
Democratic, March 4, 1857 – March 4, 1861

Inaugural Address, March 4, 1857

America, at its best,
is also courageous.

GEORGE W. BUSH (43RD)
Republican, January 20, 2001 – January 20, 2009

Inaugural Address, January 20, 2001

[America's] glory is not dominion,
but liberty.

JOHN QUINCY ADAMS (6ᵀᴴ)
Democratic-Republican, March 4, 1825 – March 4, 1829

**Speech to the US House of Representatives on
foreign policy, July 4, 1821**

"

It is inspiring, too, to remember that no great emergency in the one hundred and eight years of our eventful national life has ever arisen that has not been met with wisdom and courage by the American people, with fidelity to their best interests and highest destiny, and to the honor of the American name.

"

WILLIAM McKINLEY (25TH)
Republican, March 4, 1897 – September 14, 1901

First Inaugural Address, March 4, 1897

I can express no better hope for my country than that the kind Providence which smiled upon our fathers may enable their children to preserve the blessings they have inherited.

FRANKLIN PIERCE (14TH)
Democratic, March 4, 1853 – March 4, 1857

Inaugural Address, March 4, 1853

66

Under this Constitution the boundaries of freedom have been enlarged, the foundations of order and peace have been strengthened, and the growth of our people in all the better elements of national life has indicated the wisdom of the founders and given new hope to their descendants.

99

JAMES A. GARFIELD (20TH)
Republican, March 4, 1881 – September 19, 1881

Inaugural Address, March 4, 1881

No other theory is adequate to explain or comprehend the Declaration of Independence. It is the product of the spiritual insight of the people. We live in an age of science and of abounding accumulation of material things. These did not create our Declaration. Our Declaration created them.

CALVIN COOLIDGE (30TH)
Republican, August 2, 1923 – March 4, 1929

"The Inspiration of the Declaration" speech, July 5, 1926

"

Two centuries ago our Nation's birth was a milestone in the long quest for freedom, but the bold and brilliant dream which excited the founders of this Nation still awaits its consummation. I have no new dream to set forth today, but rather urge a fresh faith in the old dream.

"

JIMMY CARTER (39TH)
Democratic, January 20, 1977 – January 20, 1981

Inauguration Address, January 20, 1977

CHAPTER
TWO

The Constitution set out to
represent the values
of the American people and it is
the duty of the President
to represent the people in the
United States.

WE THE PEOPLE

Throughout our history the American people have always been the true source of American greatness.

DONALD TRUMP (45TH)
Republican, January 20, 2017 – Incumbent

Security strategy speech, December 18, 2017

We must do what America does best: offer more opportunity to all and demand more responsibility from all.

BILL CLINTON (42ND)
Democratic, January 20, 1993 – January 20, 2001

First Inaugural Address, January 20, 1993

No President, no government, can teach us to remember what is best in what we are.

GEORGE H. W. BUSH (41ST)
Republican, January 20, 1989 – January 20, 1993

Inaugural Address, January 20, 1989

System in all things is the soul of business. To deliberate maturely, & execute promptly is the way to conduct it to advantage. With me, it has always been a maxim, rather to let my designs appear from my works, than by my expressions.

GEORGE WASHINGTON (1ST)
Unaffiliated, April 30, 1789 – March 4, 1797

Letter to James Anderson, December 21, 1797

The stars upon your banner have become nearly threefold their original number; your densely populated possessions skirt the shores of the two great oceans; and yet this vast increase of people and territory … has afforded an additional guaranty of the strength and integrity of both.

FRANKLIN PIERCE (14TH)
Democratic, March 4, 1853 – March 4, 1857

Inaugural Address, March 4, 1853

Greatness comes in simple trappings.

RICHARD NIXON (37TH)
Republican, January 20, 1969 – August 9, 1974

First Inaugural Address, January 20, 1969

I do not mistrust the future; I do not fear what is ahead. For our problems are large, but our heart is larger. Our challenges are great, but our will is greater.

GEORGE H. W. BUSH (41ST)
Republican, January 20, 1989 – January 20, 1993

Inaugural Address, January 20, 1989

Every difference of opinion, is not a difference of principle. We have called by different names brethren of the same principle. We are all republicans: we are all federalists.

THOMAS JEFFERSON (3ᴿᴰ)
Democratic-Republican, March 4, 1801 – March 4, 1809

First Inaugural Address, March 4, 1801

Powerful people maneuver for position and worry endlessly about who is in and who is out, who is up and who is down, forgetting those people whose toil and sweat sends us here and pays our way.

BILL CLINTON (42ND)
Democratic, January 20, 1993 – January 20, 2001

First Inaugural Address, January 20, 1993

There is but one just use of power,
and it is to serve people.

GEORGE H. W. BUSH (41ST)
Republican, January 20, 1989 – January 20, 1993

Inaugural Address, January 20, 1989

Enlightenment must be accompanied by that moral power which is the product of the home and of rebellion. Real education and true welfare for the people rest inevitably on this foundation, which the Government can approve and commend, but which the people themselves must create.

CALVIN COOLIDGE (30TH)
Republican, August 2, 1923 – March 4, 1929

First Annual Message to the Congress, December 6, 1923

The shadows that now lie dark upon our path will soon be dispelled, and we shall walk with the light all about us if we be but true to ourselves...

WOODROW WILSON (28TH)
Democratic, March 4, 1913 – March 4, 1921

Second Inaugural Address, March 5, 1917

Institutions like ours, in which all power is derived directly from the people, must depend mainly upon their intelligence, patriotism, and industry.

ULYSSES S. GRANT (18TH)
Republican, March 4, 1869 – March 4, 1877

Announcement of Fifteenth Amendment Ratification, March 30, 1870

Knowledge is in every country the surest basis of public happiness.

GEORGE WASHINGTON (1ST)
Unaffiliated, April 30, 1789 – March 4, 1797

First Annual Address, January 8, 1790

Americans are generous and strong and decent, not because we believe in ourselves, but because we hold beliefs beyond ourselves. When this spirit of citizenship is missing, no government program can replace it. When this spirit is present, no wrong can stand against it.

GEORGE W. BUSH (43RD)
Republican, January 20, 2001 – January 20, 2009

First Inaugural Address, January 20, 2001

There are, perhaps, few men who can for any great length of time enjoy office and power without being more or less under the influence of feelings unfavorable to the faithful discharge of their public duties.

ANDREW JACKSON (7TH)
Democratic, March 4, 1829 – March 4, 1837

First Annual Message, December 8, 1829

On my desk in the Oval Office, I have a little sign that says: 'There is no limit to what a man can do or where he can go if he doesn't mind who gets the credit.'

RONALD REAGAN (40TH)
Republican, January 20, 1981 – January 20, 1989

Remarks at a Meeting of the White House Conference for a Drug Free America, February 29, 1988

America has never been united by blood or birth or soil. We are bound by ideals that move us beyond our backgrounds, lift us above our interests and teach us what it means to be citizens.

GEORGE W. BUSH (43ᴿᴰ)
Republican, January 20, 2001 – January 20, 2009

First Inaugural Address, January 20, 2001

If we succeed, it will not be because of what we have, but it will be because of what we are; not because of what we own, but, rather because of what we believe.

LYNDON B. JOHNSON (36TH)
Democratic, November 22, 1963 – January 20, 1969

First Inaugural Address, January 20, 1965

66

We all do better when we
work together. Our differences
do matter, but our common
humanity matters more.

99

BILL CLINTON (42ND)
Democratic, January 20, 1993 – January 20, 2001

Little Rock, Arkansas, November 19, 2004

Our Government springs from and was made for the people – not the people for the Government.

ANDREW JOHNSON (17TH)
National Union, April 15, 1865 – March 4, 1869

First Annual Message, December 4, 1865

66

...this nation is its own judge when to accord the rights of belligerency...

ULYSSES S. GRANT (18TH)
Republican, March 4, 1869 – March 4, 1877

First Annual Message, December 6, 1869

No country is more loved by its people. I have an abiding faith in their capacity, integrity and high purpose. I have no fears for the future of our country. It is bright with hope.

HERBERT HOOVER (31ST)
Republican, March 4, 1929 – March 4, 1933

Inaugural Address, March 4, 1929

America, at its best, matches a
commitment to principle with a
concern for civility.

GEORGE W. BUSH (43RD)
Republican, January 20, 2001 – January 20, 2009

First Inaugural Address, January 20, 2001

Freedom, by its nature, must be chosen, and defended by citizens, and sustained by the rule of law and the protection of minorities.

GEORGE W. BUSH (43RD)
Republican, January 20, 2001 – January 20, 2009

Second Inaugural Address, January 20, 2005

…he serves his party best who serves the country best.

RUTHERFORD B. HAYES (19TH)
Republican, March 4, 1877 – March 4, 1881

Inaugural Address, March 5, 1877

What is needed now, more than ever, is leadership that steers us away from fear and fosters greater confidence in the inherent goodness and ingenuity of humanity.

JIMMY CARTER (39TH)
Democratic, January 20, 1977 – January 20, 1981

"**A Time for Peace: Rejecting Violence to Secure Human Rights**" **speech, The Carter Center, Atlanta, June 21, 2016**

We cannot learn from one another until we stop shouting at one another – until we speak quietly enough so that our words can be heard as well as our voices.

RICHARD NIXON (37TH)
Republican, January 20, 1969 – August 9, 1974

First Inaugural Address, January 20, 1969

The object of government is the welfare of the people.

THEODORE ROOSEVELT (26TH)
Republican, September 14, 1901 – March 4, 1909

"The New Nationalism" speech, Osawatomie, Kansas, August 31, 1910

Eventually, the call of
freedom comes to every
mind and every soul.

GEORGE W. BUSH (43RD)
Republican, January 20, 2001 – January 20, 2009

Second Inaugural Address, January 20, 2005

The strong man who in the confidence of sturdy health courts the sternest activities of life and rejoices in the hardihood of constant labor may still have lurking near his vitals the unheeded disease that dooms him to sudden collapse.

GROVER CLEVELAND (24TH)
Democratic, March 4, 1893 – March 4, 1897

Second Inaugural Address, March 4, 1893

A regret for the mistakes of yesterday must not, however, blind us to the tasks of today.

WARREN G. HARDING (29TH)
Republican, March 4, 1921 – August 2, 1923

Inaugural Address, March 4, 1921

The American people, entrenched in freedom at home, take their love for it with them wherever they go...

WILLIAM McKINLEY (25TH)
Republican, March 4, 1897 – September 14, 1901

Second Inaugural Address, March 4, 1901

"

There is a power in public opinion in this country – and I thank God for it: for it is the most honest and best of all powers – which will not tolerate an incompetent or unworthy man to hold in his weak or wicked hands the lives and fortunes of his fellow-citizens.

"

MARTIN VAN BUREN (8TH)
Democratic, March 4, 1837 – March 4, 1841

Senate Speech on the Judiciary, April 7, 1826

Democracy belongs to us all, and freedom is like a beautiful kite that can go higher and higher with the breeze.

GEORGE H. W. BUSH (41ST)
Republican, January 20, 1989 – January 20, 1993

Inaugural Address, January 20, 1989

"

We must adjust to changing
times and still hold to unchanging
principles.

"

JIMMY CARTER (39TH)
Democratic, January 20, 1977 – January 20, 1981

Inaugural Address, January 20, 1977

Through times of war and
peace and many changes
of administration, the constant
has been the diplomatic policy of
the President to represent the
best interests of the American
people on the global stage.

BIG STICK DIPLOMACY

I can never consent to being dictated to.

99

JOHN TYLER (10TH)
Whig, April 4, 1841 – March 4, 1845

Quoted in Philip Abbott, *Accidental Presidents*, 2008

From this day forward, it's going to be only America first. America first. Every decision on trade, on taxes, on immigration, on foreign affairs will be made to benefit American workers and American families.

DONALD TRUMP (45TH)
Republican, January 20, 2017 – Incumbent

Inaugural Address, January 20, 2017

Turning our eyes to other nations, our great desire is to see our brethren of the human race secured in the blessings enjoyed by ourselves, and advancing in knowledge, in freedom, and in social happiness.

ANDREW JACKSON (7ᵀᴴ)
Democratic, March 4, 1829 – March 4, 1837

First Annual Message, December 8, 1829

Our country has one cardinal principle to maintain in its foreign policy. It is an American principle. It must be an American policy. We attend to our own affairs, conserve our own strength, and protect the interests of our own citizens; but we recognize thoroughly our obligation to help others, reserving to the decision of our own Judgment the time, the place, and the method.

CALVIN COOLIDGE (30TH)
Republican, August 2, 1923 – March 4, 1929

First Annual Message to the Congress, December 6, 1923

Our vast world responsibility accents with urgency our people's elemental right to a government whose clear qualities are loyalty, security, efficiency, economy, and integrity.

DWIGHT D. EISENHOWER (34TH)
Republican, January 20, 1953 – January 20, 1961

1953 State of the Union Address

The anchor in our world today is freedom, holding us steady in times of change, a symbol of hope to all the world.

GEORGE H. W. BUSH (41ST)
Republican, January 20, 1989 – January 20, 1993

State of the Union Address, January 31, 1990

Next to being right, it is important to Governments, as well as individuals, to be consistent.

MARTIN VAN BUREN (8TH)
Democratic, March 4, 1837 – March 4, 1841

Senate speech on the Panama mission, March 14, 1826

66

Nations, like individuals in a state of nature, are equal and independent, possessing certain rights and owing certain duties to each other, arising from their necessary and unavoidable relations; which rights and duties there is no common human authority to protect and enforce.

99

MILLARD FILLMORE (13TH)
Whig, July 9, 1850 – March 4, 1853

First Annual Message, December 2, 1850

My fellow Americans, let us take that first step. Let us... step back from the shadow of war and seek out the way of peace. And if that journey is a thousand miles, or even more, let history record that we, in this land, at this time, took the first step.

JOHN F. KENNEDY (35TH)
Democratic, January 20, 1961 – November 22, 1963

Radio and television address to the American People on the Nuclear Test Ban Treaty, July 26, 1963

We know what works: Freedom works. We know what's right: Freedom is right.

GEORGE H. W. BUSH (41ST)
Republican, January 20, 1989 – January 20, 1993

Inaugural Address, January 20, 1989

Our democracy must be not only the envy of the world but the engine of our own renewal. There is nothing wrong with America that cannot be cured by what is right with America.

BILL CLINTON (42ND)
Democratic, January 20, 1993 – January 20, 2001

First Inaugural Address, January 20, 1993

"

Our Nation can be strong abroad
only if it is strong at home.

"

JIMMY CARTER (39TH)
Democratic, January 20, 1977 – January 20, 1981

Inaugural Address, January 20, 1977

Successful foreign policy is an extension of the hopes of the whole American people for a world of peace and orderly reform and orderly freedom.

GERALD R. FORD (38TH)
Republican, August 9, 1974 – January 20, 1977

Address to a Joint Session of the Congress, August 12, 1974

66

This is one of those times in the affairs of nations when the gravest choices must be made, if there is to be a turning toward a just and lasting peace.

99

DWIGHT D. EISENHOWER (34TH)
Republican, January 20, 1953 – January 20, 1961

"The Chance for Peace" address delivered before the American Society of Newspaper Editors, Statler Hotel, Washington DC, April 16, 1953

Internal improvement and the diffusion of knowledge, so far as they can be promoted by the constitutional acts of the Federal Government, are of high importance.

ANDREW JACKSON (7TH)
Democratic, March 4, 1829 – March 4, 1837

Inaugural Address, March 4, 1829

66

To Iran and to Russia, I ask:
what kind of nation wants to be
associated with the mass murder
of innocent men, women and
children? The nations of the world
can be judged by the friends they
keep. No nation can succeed
in the long run by promoting
rogue states, brutal tyrants, and
murderous dictators.

99

DONALD TRUMP (45TH)
Republican, January 20, 2017 – Incumbent

Televised address to the nation, April 13, 2018

The survival of liberty in our land increasingly depends on the success of liberty in other lands. The best hope for peace in our world is the expansion of freedom in all the world.

GEORGE W. BUSH (43RD)
Republican, January 20, 2001 – January 20, 2009

Second Inaugural Address, January 20, 2005

66

The whole art of government consists in the art of being honest.

99

THOMAS JEFFERSON (3RD)
Democratic-Republican, March 4, 1801 – March 4, 1809

**"A Summary View of the Rights of British America",
July 1774**

We are a purely idealistic Nation,
but let no one confuse our idealism
with weakness.

JIMMY CARTER (39TH)
Democratic, January 20, 1977 – January 20, 1981

Inaugural Address, January 20, 1977

We not only desire peace with the world, but to see peace maintained throughout the world. We wish to advance the reign of justice and reason toward the extinction of force.

HERBERT HOOVER (31ST)
Republican, March 4, 1929 – March 4, 1933

Inaugural Address, March 4, 1929

When our vital interests are challenged or the will and conscience of the international community is defied, we will act, with peaceful diplomacy whenever possible, with force when necessary.

BILL CLINTON (42ND)
Democratic, January 20, 1993 – January 20, 2001

First Inaugural Address, January 20, 1993

Great nations like great men must keep their word.

GEORGE H. W. BUSH (41ST)
Republican, January 20, 1989 – January 20, 1993

Inaugural Address, January 20, 1989

Let us never negotiate out
of fear. But let us never fear
to negotiate.

JOHN F. KENNEDY (35TH)
Democratic, January 20, 1961 – November 22, 1963

Inaugural Address, January 20, 1961

Our eyes never will be blind to a developing menace, our ears never deaf to the call of civilization. **"**

WARREN G. HARDING (29TH)
Republican, March 4, 1921 – August 2, 1923

Inaugural Address, March 4, 1921

The enemies of liberty and our country should make no mistake, America remains engaged in the world by history and by choice, shaping a balance of power that favors freedom.

GEORGE W. BUSH (43RD)
Republican, January 20, 2001 – January 20, 2009

Inaugural Address, January 20, 2001

66

Speak softly and carry a big stick –
you will go far.

99

THEODORE ROOSEVELT (26TH)
Republican, September 14, 1901 – March 4, 1909

Minnesota State Fair, September 2, 1901

Calmness, justice, and consideration should characterize our diplomacy.

BENJAMIN HARRISON (23RD)
Republican, March 4, 1889 – March 4, 1893

Inaugural Address, March 4, 1889

All this will not be finished in the first one hundred days. Nor will it be finished in the first one thousand days, not in the life of this Administration, nor even perhaps in our lifetime on this planet. But let us begin.

JOHN F. KENNEDY (35TH)
Democratic, January 20, 1961 – November 22, 1963

Inaugural Address, January 20, 1961

CHAPTER
FOUR

The great responsibility of the Executive branch is to unite the nation, offering guidance and leadership while holding office.

WHAT YOU CAN DO FOR YOUR COUNTRY

Mothers and children trapped in poverty in our inner cities, rusted out factories, scattered like tombstones across the landscape of our nation, an education system flush with cash, but which leaves our young and beautiful students deprived of all knowledge…

…and the crime, and the gangs, and the drugs that have stolen too many lives and robbed our country of so much unrealized potential. This American carnage stops right here and stops right now. 🙶

DONALD TRUMP (45TH)
Republican, January 20, 2017 – Incumbent

Inaugural Address, January 20, 2017

I don't think any President ever enjoyed himself more than I did… I have enjoyed my life and my work because I thoroughly believe that success – the real success – does not depend upon the position you hold, but upon how you carry yourself in that position.

THEODORE ROOSEVELT (26TH)
Republican, September 14, 1901 – March 4, 1909

An address at the Cambridge Union, May 26, 1910

We cannot claim that our Government is perfect, but we have the right to believe that it is the best that there is.

CALVIN COOLIDGE (30TH)
Republican, August 2, 1923 – March 4, 1929

Dedicating a monument to the First Division, American Expeditionary Forces, Washington DC, October 4, 1924

If one voice can change a room, then it can change a city, and if it can change a city, it can change a state, and if it can change a state, it can change a nation, and if it can change a nation, it can change the world.

BARACK OBAMA (44TH)
Democratic, January 20, 2009 – January 20, 2017

Hillary Clinton campaign rally, Durham, New Hampshire, November 2016

66

The safety of America and the trust of the people alike demand that the personnel of the Federal Government be loyal in their motives and reliable in the discharge of their duties. Only a combination of both loyalty and reliability promises genuine security.

99

DWIGHT D. EISENHOWER (34TH)
Republican, January 20, 1953 – January 20, 1961

1953 State of the Union Address

The form of government which communicates ease, comfort, security, or, in one word, happiness, to the greatest number of persons, and in the greatest degree, is the best.

JOHN ADAMS (2ND)
Federalist, March 4, 1797 – March 4, 1801

Thoughts on Government, 1776

66

I have now done my duty to my country. If sustained by my fellow citizens, I shall be grateful and happy; if not, I shall find in the motives which impel me ample grounds for contentment and peace.

99

ANDREW JACKSON (7TH)
Democratic, March 4, 1829 – March 4, 1837

Inaugural Address, March 4, 1829

I am conscious that the position which I have been called to fill, though sufficient to satisfy the loftiest ambition, is surrounded by fearful responsibilities.

ZACHARY TAYLOR (12TH)
Whig, March 4, 1849 – July 9, 1850

Inaugural Address, March 5, 1849

"

...I am certain that after the dust of centuries has passed over our cities, we, too, will be remembered not for victories or defeats in battle or in politics, but for our contribution to the human spirit.

"

JOHN F. KENNEDY (35TH)
Democratic, January 20, 1961 – November 22, 1963

Remarks at a closed-circuit television broadcast on behalf of the National Cultural Center, November 29, 1962

America has need of idealism and courage, because we have essential work at home – the unfinished work of American freedom. In a world moving toward liberty, we are determined to show the meaning and promise of liberty.

GEORGE W. BUSH (43RD)
Republican, January 20, 2001 – January 20, 2009

Second Inaugural Address, January 20, 2005

Government's first duty is to protect the people, not run their lives.

RONALD REAGAN (40TH)
Republican, January 20, 1981 – January 20, 1989

Address before a Joint Session of the Tennessee State Legislature, March 15, 1982

Democracy is based on the conviction that man has the moral and intellectual capacity, as well as the inalienable right, to govern himself with reason and justice.

HARRY S. TRUMAN (33RD)
Democratic, April 12, 1945 – January 20, 1953

Second Inaugural Address, January 20, 1949

"

Each moment in history is a fleeting time, precious and unique. But some stand out as moments of beginning, in which courses are set that shape decades or centuries. This can be such a moment.

"

RICHARD NIXON (37TH)
Republican, January 20, 1969 – August 9, 1974

First Inaugural Address, January 20, 1969

You have given me a great responsibility – to stay close to you, to be worthy of you, and to exemplify what you are. Let us create together a new national spirit of unity and trust. Your strength can compensate for my weakness, and your wisdom can help to minimize my mistakes.

JIMMY CARTER (39TH)
Democratic, January 20, 1977 – January 20, 1981

Inaugural Address, January 20, 1977

66

They know that a government
big enough to give you everything
you want is a government
big enough to take from you
everything you have.

99

GERALD R. FORD (38TH)
Republican, August 9, 1974 – January 20, 1977

**Address to a Joint Session of the Congress,
August 12, 1974**

Change does not come from Washington, but to Washington.

BARACK OBAMA (44TH)
Democratic, January 20, 2009 – January 20, 2017

Let Freedom Ring ceremony on the 50th anniversary of the March on Washington, August 28, 2013

Faith in the people does not mean faith in a part of the people. It means faith in all the people. Our country is always safe when decisions are made by a majority of those who are entitled to vote. It is always in peril when decisions are made by a minority.

CALVIN COOLIDGE (30TH)
Republican, August 2, 1923 – March 4, 1929

Radio address from the White House, November 3, 1924

There would be little traffic in illegal liquor if only criminals patronized it. We must awake to the fact that this patronage from large numbers of law-abiding citizens is supplying the rewards and stimulating crime.

HERBERT HOOVER (31ST)
Republican, March 4, 1929 – March 4, 1933

Inaugural Address, March 4, 1929

Blessed as our country is with every thing which constitutes national strength, she is fully adequate to the maintenance of all her interests.

ANDREW JACKSON (7TH)
Democratic, March 4, 1829 – March 4, 1837

First Annual Message, December 8, 1829

> In the Chinese language, the word 'crisis' is composed of two characters, one representing danger and the other, opportunity.

JOHN F. KENNEDY (35TH)
Democratic, January 20, 1961 – November 22, 1963

Speech at United Negro College Fund fundraiser, Indianapolis, Indiana, April 12, 1959

" Renewed in our strength – tested, but not weary – we are ready for the greatest achievements in the history of freedom. "

GEORGE W. BUSH (43RD)
Republican, January 20, 2001 – January 20, 2009

Second Inaugural Address, January 20, 2005

The unselfishness of these United States is a thing proven; our devotion to peace for ourselves and for the world is well established; our concern for preserved civilization has had its impassioned and heroic expression. There was no American failure to resist the attempted reversion of civilization; there will be no failure today or tomorrow.

WARREN G. HARDING (29TH)
Republican, March 4, 1921 – August 2, 1923

Inaugural Address, March 4, 1921

...we can have peace.
The initiative is ours.

HARRY S. TRUMAN (33RD)
Democratic, April 12, 1945 – January 20, 1953

Second Inaugural Address, January 20, 1949

We must act today in order to preserve tomorrow. And let there be no misunderstanding – we are going to begin to act, beginning today.

RONALD REAGAN (40TH)
Republican, January 20, 1981 – January 20, 1989

First Inaugural Address, January 20, 1981

Just as America's will for peace is second to none, so will America's strength be second to none.

GERALD R. FORD (38TH)
Republican, August 9, 1974 – January 20, 1977

Address to a Joint Session of the Congress, August 12, 1974

No man can be fully free while his neighbor is not. To go forward at all is to go forward together.

RICHARD NIXON (37TH)
Republican, January 20, 1969 – August 9, 1974

First Inaugural Address, January 20, 1969

"

Anyone who has taken the oath I have just taken must feel a heavy weight of responsibility. If not, he has no conception of the powers and duties of the office upon which he is about to enter, or he is lacking in a proper sense of the obligation which the oath imposes.

"

WILLIAM HOWARD TAFT (27TH)
Republican, March 4, 1909 – March 4, 1913

Inaugural Address, March 4, 1909

…what we have achieved in liberty, we will surpass in greater liberty.

HARRY S. TRUMAN (33RD)
Democratic, April 12, 1945 – January 20, 1953

Second Inaugural Address, January 20, 1949

66

Ask not what your country can do for you … ask what you can do for your country.

99

JOHN F. KENNEDY (35TH)
Democratic, January 20, 1961 – November 22, 1963

Inaugural Address, January 20, 1961

I once told you that I am not a saint, and I hope never to see the day that I cannot admit having made a mistake.

GERALD R. FORD (38TH)
Republican, August 9, 1974 – January 20, 1977

Address to a Joint Session of the Congress, August 12, 1974

66

All great change in America begins
at the dinner table.

99

RONALD REAGAN (40TH)
Republican, January 20, 1981 – January 20, 1989

Farewell to the Nation Address, January 11, 1989

Let us not despair but act.

JOHN F. KENNEDY (35TH)
Democratic, January 20, 1961 – November 22, 1963

Speech at Loyola College Alumni Banquet, Baltimore, Maryland, February 18, 1958

If citizens do not like a law, their duty as honest men and women is to discourage its violation; their right is openly to work for its repeal.

HERBERT HOOVER (31ST)
Republican, March 4, 1929 – March 4, 1933

Inaugural Address, March 4, 1929

Strong hearts and helpful hands are needed, and, fortunately, we have them in every part of our beloved country.

WILLIAM McKINLEY (25TH)
Republican, March 4, 1897 – September 14, 1901

We had revealed to us in our time of peril not only the geographical unity of our country, but... the unity of the spirit of our people. They might speak with different tongues, come from most divergent quarters of the globe, but in the essentials of the hour they were moved by a common purpose, devoted to a common cause, and loyal to a common country. **"**

CALVIN COOLIDGE (30TH)
Republican, August 2, 1923 – March 4, 1929

Armistice Day Address, dedicating Liberty Memorial in Kansas City, Missouri, November 11, 1926

CHAPTER
FIVE

As the Commander-in-Chief
the President must lead the
nation in times of war in order
to find peace.

THE ROCKET'S
RED GLARE

Yesterday, December 7th 1941, a date which will live in infamy, the United States of America was suddenly and deliberately attacked.

FRANKLIN D. ROOSEVELT (32ND)
Democratic, March 4, 1933 – April 12, 1945

Address to the Congress asking that a state of war be declared between the United States and Japan, December 8, 1941

Courageous Patriots have fought and died for our great American flag – we MUST honor and respect it!

DONALD TRUMP (45TH)
Republican, January 20, 2017 – Incumbent

Twitter, September 24, 2017

If there is not the war, you don't get the great general; if there is not a great occasion you don't get the great statesman; if Lincoln had lived in times of peace no one would have known his name now. The great crisis must come, or no man has the chance to develop great qualities.

THEODORE ROOSEVELT (26TH)
Republican, September 14, 1901 – March 4, 1909

An address at the Cambridge Union, May 26, 1910

66

It was Lincoln who pointed out that both sides prayed to the same God. When that is the case, it is only a matter of time when each will seek a common end. We can now see clearly what that end is. It is the maintenance of our American form of government, of our American institutions, of our American ideals, beneath a common flag, under the blessings of Almighty God.

99

CALVIN COOLIDGE (30TH)
Republican, August 2, 1923 – March 4, 1929

Arlington National Cemetery, Virginia, May 25, 1924

Freedom is not an accident. Progress is not an accident. Democracy is not an accident. These are things that have to be fought for.

BARACK OBAMA (44TH)
Democratic, January 20, 2009 – January 20, 2017

US Army Garrison Yongsan, Seoul, Republic of Korea, April 2014

We have learned that the free world cannot indefinitely remain in a posture of paralyzed tension, leaving forever to the aggressor the choice of time and place and means to cause greatest hurt to us at least cost to himself.

DWIGHT D. EISENHOWER (34TH)
Republican, January 20, 1953 – January 20, 1961

1953 State of the Union Address

Every post is honorable in which a man can serve his country.

GEORGE WASHINGTON (1ST)
Unaffiliated, April 30, 1789 – March 4, 1797

Letter to Benedict Arnold, September 14, 1775

I must study Politics and War that my sons may have liberty to study Mathematics and Philosophy.

JOHN ADAMS (2ND)
Federalist, March 4, 1797 – March 4, 1801

Letter to Abigail Adams, May 12, 1780

I hold it that a little rebellion now and then is a good thing, and as necessary in the political world as storms in the physical.

THOMAS JEFFERSON (3RD)
Democratic-Republican, March 4, 1801 – March 4, 1809

Letter to James Madison, January 30, 1787

Peace is not the absence of conflict, but the ability to cope with conflict by peaceful means.

RONALD REAGAN (40TH)
Republican, January 20, 1981 – January 20, 1989

Commencement Address, Eureka College, May 9, 1982

A generous country will
never forget the services
you rendered…

WARREN G. HARDING (29TH)
Republican, March 4, 1921 – August 2, 1923

Inaugural Address, March 4, 1921

The great objects of our pursuit as a people are best to be attained by peace, and are entirely consistent with the tranquillity and interests of the rest of mankind.

FRANKLIN PIERCE (14TH)
Democratic, March 4, 1853 – March 4, 1857

Inaugural Address, March 4, 1853

No matter how long it may take us to overcome this premeditated invasion, the American people in their righteous might will win through to absolute victory.

FRANKLIN D. ROOSEVELT (32ND)
Democratic, March 4, 1933 – April 12, 1945

Address to the Congress asking that a state of war be declared between the United States and Japan, December 8, 1941

66

The world will little note, nor long remember what we say here, but it can never forget what they did here.

ABRAHAM LINCOLN (16TH)
National Union, March 4, 1861 – April 15, 1865

Gettysburg Address, November 19, 1863

Great harm has been done to us. We have suffered great loss. And in our grief and anger we have found our mission and our moment. Freedom and fear are at war. The advance of human freedom – the great achievement of our time, and the great hope of every time – now depends on us.

GEORGE W. BUSH (43RD)
Republican, January 20, 2001 – January 20, 2009

State of the Union Address, September 19, 2001

Freedom is never more than one generation away from extinction. It has to be fought for and defended by each generation.

RONALD REAGAN (40TH)
Republican, January 20, 1981 – January 20, 1989

Annual Convention of Kiwanis International, July 6, 1987

This is not a day of triumph;
it is a day of dedication…
I summon all honest men, all
patriotic, all forward-looking
men, to my side.

WOODROW WILSON (28TH)
Democratic, March 4, 1913 – March 4, 1921

First Inaugural Address, March 4, 1913

"

Freedom is not given, it
must be won, through struggle
and discipline, persistence
and faith.

"

BARACK OBAMA (44ᵀᴴ)
Democratic, January 20, 2009 – January 20, 2017

**Let Freedom Ring ceremony on the 50th anniversary
of the March on Washington, August 28, 2013**

Every unit of the American Army, whether at home or abroad, richly merits its own full measure of recognition. They shrank from no toil, no danger and no hardship, that the liberties of our country might adequately be defended and preserved.

CALVIN COOLIDGE (30TH)
Republican, August 2, 1923 – March 4, 1929

Dedicating a monument to the First Division, American Expeditionary Forces, Washington DC , October 4, 1924

66

The peace we seek, rounded upon decent trust and cooperative effort among nations, can be fortified, not by weapons of war but by wheat and by cotton, by milk and by wool, by meat and by timber and by rice. These are words that translate into every language on earth.

99

DWIGHT D. EISENHOWER (34TH)
Republican, January 20, 1953 – January 20, 1961

"The Chance for Peace" address delivered before the American Society of Newspaper Editors, Statler Hotel, Washington DC, April 16, 1953

A man who is good enough to shed his blood for his country is good enough to be given a square deal afterwards. More than that no man is entitled, and less than that no man shall have.

THEODORE ROOSEVELT (26TH)
Republican, September 14, 1901 – March 4, 1909

Speech to veterans, Springfield, Illinois, July 4, 1903

The successful warrior is no longer entitled to... fame... To be esteemed eminently great it is necessary to be eminently good. The qualities of the general and the hero must be devoted to the advantage of mankind.

WILLIAM HENRY HARRISON (9TH)
Whig, March 4, 1841 – April 4, 1841

Quoted in A. E. Hotchner, *The New York Times*, October 8, 1995

Our obligations to our country
never cease but with our lives.

JOHN ADAMS (2ND)
Federalist, March 4, 1797 – March 4, 1801

Letter to Benjamin Rush, 18 April 1808

With confidence in our armed forces with the unbounding determination of our people we will gain the inevitable triumph so help us God.

FRANKLIN D. ROOSEVELT (32ND)
Democratic, March 4, 1933 – April 12, 1945

Address to the Congress asking that a state of war be declared between the United States and Japan, December 8, 1941

Terrorism is the preferred weapon of weak and evil men.

RONALD REAGAN (40TH)
Republican, January 20, 1981 – January 20, 1989

Remarks at a meeting with members of the American Business Conference, April 15, 1986

…the great task remaining before us – that from these honored dead we take increased devotion to that cause for which they gave the last full measure of devotion – …that this nation, under God, shall have a new birth of freedom – and that government of the people, by the people, and for the people, shall not perish from the earth.

ABRAHAM LINCOLN (16TH)
National Union, March 4, 1861 – April 15, 1865

Gettysburg Address, November 19, 1863

The peace we seek in the world is not the flimsy peace which is merely an interlude between wars, but a peace which can endure for generations to come.

RICHARD NIXON (37TH)
Republican, January 20, 1969 – August 9, 1974

Second Inaugural Address, January 20, 1973

Mankind must put an end to war or war will put an end to mankind.

JOHN F. KENNEDY (35TH)
Democratic, January 20, 1961 – November 22, 1963

Address before the United Nations General Assembly, September 25, 1961

CHAPTER
SIX

The role of President is as diverse as the people who have held office, and their words represent their own unique experiences.

LIFE, LIBERTY & THE PURSUIT OF HAPPINESS

To be good, and to do good, is all
We have to do.

JOHN ADAMS (2ND)
Federalist, March 4, 1797 – March 4, 1801

Letter to Abigail Adams, March 17, 1777

66

Hope is a bedrock of this nation.
The belief that our destiny will not
be written for us, but by us, by all
those men and women who are not
content to settle for the world as it
is, who have the courage to remake
the world as It should be.

99

BARACK OBAMA (44TH)
Democratic, January 20, 2009 – January 20, 2017

Iowa caucus victory speech, January 2008

66

Error of opinion may be
tolerated, where reason is left
free to combat it.

99

THOMAS JEFFERSON (3RD)
Democratic-Republican, March 4, 1801 – March 4, 1809

First Inaugural Address, March 4, 1801

"

From the experience of the past we derive instructive lessons for the future.

"

JOHN QUINCY ADAMS (6TH)
Democratic-Republican, March 4, 1825 – March 4, 1829

Inaugural Address, March 4, 1825

If more politicians knew poetry,
and more poets knew politics,
I am convinced the world would
be a little better place in which
to live.

JOHN F. KENNEDY (35TH)
Democratic, January 20, 1961 – November 22, 1963

**Speech at Harvard University, Cambridge,
Massachusetts, June 14, 1956**

172

66

We will not tire, we will not falter, and we will not fail.

GEORGE W. BUSH (43RD)
Republican, January 20, 2001 – January 20, 2009

State of the Union Address, September 19, 2001

99

The future doesn't belong to
the fainthearted; it belongs to
the brave.

RONALD REAGAN (40TH)
Republican, January 20, 1981 – January 20, 1989

**Address to the nation on the explosion of the Space
Shuttle Challenger, January 28, 1986**

66

The American dream does not come to those who fall asleep.

99

RICHARD NIXON (37TH)
Republican, January 20, 1969 – August 9, 1974

First Inaugural Address, January 20, 1969

So long as the peoples of the world have confidence in our purposes and faith in our word, the age-old vision of peace on Earth will grow brighter.

GERALD R. FORD (38TH)
Republican, August 9, 1974 – January 20, 1977

Address to a Joint Session of the Congress, August 12, 1974

66

But all this majestic advance should not obscure the constant dangers from which self-government must be safeguarded. The strong man must at all times be alert to the attack of insidious disease.

99

HERBERT HOOVER (31ST)
Republican, March 4, 1929 – March 4, 1933

Inaugural Address, March 4, 1929

The circulation of confidence is better than the circulation of money.

JAMES MADISON (4TH)
Democratic-Republican, March 4, 1809 – March 4, 1817

The Debates in the Several State Conventions on the Adoption of the Federal Constitution, 1836

The gratitude… should be commensurate with the boundless blessings which we enjoy.

JAMES K. POLK (11TH)
Democratic, March 4, 1845 – March 4, 1849

Fourth Annual Message to Congress, December 5, 1848

Mankind needs a world-wide
benediction of understanding.

WARREN G. HARDING (29TH)
Republican, March 4, 1921 – August 2, 1923

Inaugural Address, March 4, 1921

I look forward to an America which will not be afraid of grace and beauty... an America which will reward achievement in the arts as we reward achievement in business or statecraft.

JOHN F. KENNEDY (35TH)
Democratic, January 20, 1961 – November 22, 1963

Remarks at Amherst College upon receiving an Honorary Degree, October 26, 1963

Heroes have made poets,
and poets heroes.

GEORGE WASHINGTON (1ST)
Unaffiliated, April 30, 1789 – March 4, 1797

Letter to the Marquis de Lafayette, May 28, 1788

The job-seekers pack the White House every day, pushing their applications at me – in my hands, in my pockets. They pursue me so closely that I can not even attend to the necessary functions of nature.

WILLIAM HENRY HARRISON (9TH)
Whig, March 4, 1841 – April 4, 1841

Quoted in A. E. Hotchner, *The New York Times*, October 8, 1995

Our democratic faith is more than
the creed of our country, it is the
inborn hope of our humanity...

GEORGE W. BUSH (43RD)
Republican, January 20, 2001 – January 20, 2009

First Inaugural Address, January 20, 2001

Our destiny offers, not the cup of despair, but the chalice of opportunity. So let us seize it...

RICHARD NIXON (37TH)
Republican, January 20, 1969 – August 9, 1974

First Inaugural Address, January 20, 1969

Men may die, but the fabrics
of our free institutions remain
unshaken.

CHESTER A. ARTHUR (21ST)
Republican, September 19, 1881 – March 4, 1885

**Address upon assuming the office of President,
September 22, 1881**

The bud of victory is always in the truth.

BENJAMIN HARRISON (23RD)
Republican, March 4, 1889 – March 4, 1893

Indianapolis Speech, September 18, 1888

If we can but prevent the government from wasting the labours of the people, under the pretence of taking care of them, they must become happy.

THOMAS JEFFERSON (3RD)
Democratic-Republican, March 4, 1801 – March 4, 1809

Letter to Thomas Cooper, November 29, 1802

"

I commit with humble but fearless confidence my own fate and the future destinies of my country. **"**

JOHN QUINCY ADAMS (6TH)
Democratic-Republican, March 4, 1825 – March 4, 1829

Inaugural Address, March 4, 1825

We must use time as a tool, not as a couch.

JOHN F. KENNEDY (35TH)
Democratic, January 20, 1961 – November 22, 1963

**Address in New York City to the National Association
of Manufacturers, December 5, 1961**

"

Balancing the budget is a little like protecting your virtue: You just have to learn to say 'no'.

"

RONALD REAGAN (40TH)
Republican, January 20, 1981 – January 20, 1989

Remarks at Kansas State University at the Alfred M. Landon Lecture Series on Public Issues, September 9, 1982

A person can be expected to
act responsibly only if he has
responsibility.

RICHARD NIXON (37ᵀᴴ)
Republican, January 20, 1969 – August 9, 1974

Second Inaugural Address, January 20, 1973